My Confession

Finding Myself
at the Feet of Jesus

By Chris Buscher

© 2015 LMDM Publishing House

Printed in the United States of America

First Printing, 2014

LMDM Publishing House

www.LMDMpublishinghouse.com

For all of those I've hurt
For all of those I've failed.
May you find the same peace now within me.

TABLE OF CONTENTS

ACKNOWLEDGEMENTS

My Father, Thomas H Buscher

You showed me the 'Father Heart of God' unconditionally throughout many years of pain. Though my actions hurt you deeply, you never gave up on me and attempted to lead me down a path of righteousness. It is my daily prayer that someday I become half the father you were to me.

My Mother, Sandra K Buscher

Having brought me into this world, an unspeakable bond has held us together no matter the distance between us. Your prayers have been heard, your faith has been accredited to you, and your miracle received. I will never forget your sacrifices that enabled me to become a man of Faith.

My beautiful wife, Jessica Buscher

You will never know how special you are or how many lives you have impacted by your generous heart. Without you by my side, I wouldn't be strong enough to walk through the many doors of faith presented before me. I love you with all of my heart; you are mine and I am yours.

My loyal friend, Thomas Doyne Jennings (LTD)

I don't know what you saw in me but I'm truly grateful that you faithfully encouraged me to follow Jesus. You became the brother I lost, the friend I needed, and the support system to which the birth of *Lay Me Down Ministry* needed to take root.

My brother, Joey

I'm sorry I hurt you and I know nothing I say or do in the future can take away the damage that was done between us. Not a day goes by that I don't thank God that you have given me another opportunity to be your brother again. No matter where life takes you or what situation you find yourself in, always remember to look to Jesus. He is there and He is more real than you or I will ever know.

My sisters: Katie Lalley, Amanda Cook, and Anne Buscher (Little Anne)

You were too young to understand and undeserving of the pain I inflicted upon you. I'm afraid my actions affected you the most, having robbed you of a normal childhood of safety and security. Yet I am extremely proud of each of you for having become champions of your careers and strong pillars of western society. Always remember no matter how large the success or security you find yourself in; we all need a savior, we all need Jesus.

My late grandmother, Barbra Buscher

I was never able to say goodbye and for that I am sorry. I know you're seated with our Creator at this very moment and proud of my actions through service to our King. You're faith, love, and words will go with me to every nation every tribe and every tongue.

Everyone my sins affected

I can't recall all of your names but the memories of my sins against you have not subdued. I cannot change my past nor the hurt I have caused, just know everything I now do, I do for you. Your memory is the fuel for this fight of faith that I refuse to lose.

The men and women of God who faithfully serve the ministry at Teen Challenge

In the entire world, there is not a more anointed God appointed ministry like that of Teen Challenge. On behalf of the multitude of us whose lives you have changed, I thank you from the bottom of my heart. I thank you. God used you to change this 'Hopeless dope addict into a dope-less hope addict'. May the Lord ever be with you.

PROLOGUE

What a wonderful thing the Lord did when He "introduced" me to Brother Chris Buscher.

Pastor Chris sent me a message a few months ago, wanting to know more information about publishing his book in Portuguese. Until that moment, I had never heard about him.

Shortly after our first meeting, the need arose for a speaker in our youth conference at the church. Even without knowing him personally, Brother Ronaldo (our youth pastor) led us to watch some of his sermons on YouTube. It did not take too long for us to understand that we were watching a man preaching out of his own experiences with the Lord.

We called him, and the whole church was excited when he accepted our humble invitation to minister at our Youth Conference. We had two nights full of God's glory and of uncommon fellowship, as if we had known each other for decades. The time we spent with Pastor Chris and his wife, Jessica, marked our lives forever.

From that weekend we knew that his testimony needed to be published. He shares his pain

5

directly: from the abuse in his childhood to the suffering he caused himself and others, he hides neither details nor moments of shame.

For the reader, your first impression might be that you are reading the story of a well-aged man that has served the Lord for some decades. But your tears will fall as you imagine the 17-year-old boy that survived each second of such a painful story. The moment Christ saved Brother Chris, your spirit will leap within as the words fly off the page and into your soul.

Chris not only found life for himself but he also found the value of serving the Master by going everywhere in world preaching the Gospel to all the people. Allow the Lord to touch your heart, build up your Faith, and implant a desire to serve. May you be forever changed as you read this beautiful testimony of our beloved brother, Pastor Chris Buscher.

Pastor Eneas Francisco,

Publisher, UP books

CHAPTER ONE:

Innocent No More

WITH MY EYES CLOSED, I can feel the pain of what is happening consumes me. As my breath quickens, I hear the sound of my heartbeat pounding in my ears. I listened to the sound of the camera snapping photos in the background, knowing that my family won't return for hours. How could they leave me with this monster? The more I fight her, the worse it becomes. I am too weak now to escape this nightmare; a nightmare I will never forget.

I hear her cold voice telling me this is punishment for being a bad child as I feel my pants and shirt being ripped away from my shaking body.

"Please stop! I won't say anything! I'll be a good boy, I promise! Please! Please! Please!" I trembled.

This was the beginning of a childhood terror that haunted me for years. A memory that burns so deep that the wound refuses to heal. It is my earliest memory, but not the most influential. This was only the beginning, the beginning of something more...

Raised in a small Midwestern city by a Catholic family, I heard about God from the Bible daily. God the Father, Jesus the Son, and the mystery of the Holy Spirit was the foundation of each story. That God, the God I always heard about, seemed unreachable and distant.

Even at an early age, I had an overwhelming curiosity about life. I can remember the night that curiosity was first peaked. One night, my father sat me down to tell me about the death of his grandmother. Although, I was too young to fully understand the meaning of death, I could feel fear rising up in my chest. While my father tried to help me understand, I slowly came to realize that someday, everyone dies. I knew I couldn't see my great grandmother anymore and I found no comfort in my father's efforts to ease my pain through this transition. During this time, I sought out the reasons for my existence on this earth and how my actions would affect life after death.

The more curious I became, the more my little world grew. I soon looked at people differently, seeing the hopelessness in their eyes while they pretended to have the answers I desperately sought. I questioned everything. I questioned everyone. I even questioned myself.

The more my family attempted to find me help coping with my terror, the more distant I became. Starting at an early age, microphones, tape recorders, and video equipment were forced in front of me demanding that I relive my childhood trauma. Hour after hour, details were forced from me. Several physiologists demanded that I explain how it felt having my innocence stolen from me. Only after I retold the story through the tears, again and again, would they then study my reactions, while I uncontrollably sobbed.

My parents never told my siblings what happened but all my extended family knew. I could see it in their eyes and through the way they treated me. They were always so careful with their words and hesitant with their reactions to my outbursts. I felt fragile. I felt different. I felt alone. I felt lost.

Throughout grammar school, I developed a split personality. It was as if two people lived inside of me. While one desperately felt the need to be loved and accepted, the other rejected everyone and constructed strong emotional walls protecting me from my unstable environment. While the educators were busy teaching, strange thoughts consumed me. I would fantasize all day about violent acts of death, ultimately leading to my own thoughts of suicide.

Even though I wasn't very talkative, every teacher quickly came to understand I was different. I received proctored testing from professionals to assess my learning capabilities. When they couldn't find a problem with me, my parents would then be called in for a parent-teacher conference. During these conferences my childhood secret always surfaced, once again reminding me of how very different I was from the other children.

For years, my "childhood secret" haunted me and hindered my emotional development, surviving through a constant state of desperation, guilt and inadequacy.

I distinctly remember my first day of middle school. Change was happening as I felt more grown up and in control of my life. Instead of having just one teacher for the whole day, now I had four. More was expected from me at school, and with the added responsibilities came more rewards. I greatly enjoyed the change of environment and quickly embraced this new found opportunity.

Throughout summer vacation, I pondered on how I could use all these changes to my advantage. I desperately desired friends and needed to be thought of as normal. After getting ideas from my favorite television programs, I decided that I would become the class clown. I believed if I could make people laugh then maybe, just maybe, they would want to be close enough that I could finally be and feel accepted.

I didn't know where to begin or how to tell my first joke. Having spent the last 12 years sheltering myself from the reality in which they lived, I soon understood this would not be an easy task. Hour after hour I would listen to comedians on my tape player writing down every word and putting it to memory. Day and night, I would gaze into my bedroom mirror scripting my jokes and alternative scenarios, preparing and waiting for my moment.

After a year of 'intense' preparation and meditation, I knew it was time. I started with my first joke in the science lab. It was the first time my classmates heard me speak more than a couple words, so naturally all eyes were on me. I felt an instant state of euphoria, followed closely by an overwhelming sense of purpose. The whole day people looked at me differently, and for once, they met my eyes and gave me attention. Though inside I wanted to cry out with a sense of relief, deep down I knew it wasn't going to last.

For the next two years I would be the school comedian. Not a comedian people respected, but a comedian who makes jokes at his own expense as self-preservation. However, I was still under the supervision of several psychologists who weekly would handle my medications, many of which were still considered experimental. Although the doctors made promise after promise, the medications did nothing but cause detrimental side effects including extreme weight gain, drowsiness, outbursts, and black outs. These side effects not only altered my life by preventing me from functioning in school, but they also hurt anyone unfortunate enough to cross my path.

I gained a lot of weight from one such medication that promised to take away my pain.

This poison imprisoned me in a constant state of drowsiness and insatiable hunger. Eating and sleeping soon became my daily life. I could do none of the physical activities I once enjoyed. By the time the doctors changed my medication it was too late. I was already obese and more depressed than before.

Sometimes my father would attempt to alleviate my feelings of depression. He would encourage me to ride my bicycle, roller blade, travel with him on business, or anything he could think of to encourage me to leave the computer or sofa behind. Unfortunately, when my father would ask, my response was never what he expected.

Something uncontrollable would take over me, something like rage, a demonic rage. I could see and understand my every action, but I had no remorse. No remorse and little self-control. Like an insignificant spark near a fuel, I would explode. Several times I would lunge at my father, trying to kill him: reaching for guns that were securely locked away, thrusting knives at him, or finding anything I could to hurt this man.

I loved him and I knew that I did, but at these moments, the ones I loved suffered the most. My eyes would roll back in my skull and the blackouts would begin. After the violent outbursts, I would wake up covered in tears and sweat only to face the destruction I created all around me. The house would be destroyed as would the relationships I had with my loved ones. On the outside, I tried to appear strong, happy, and normal but on the inside, I couldn't have been more lost. I hated myself. I hated my life. I hated my existence. I felt completely and utterly emotionally and spiritually dead.

"The godless in heart harbor resentment; even when he fetters them, they do not cry for help."

-        **Job 36:13**

CHAPTER TWO:

The Pain and Addiction

C HRIS, CAN YOU HEAR ME? Did you hear what I just told you?" said Doctor Thompson. "Chris I'm going to change your medication, they seem to be having undesired side effects."

As soon as I heard those words, I was instantly reminded of the movie 'Forest Gump', specifically the scene where he awakes one morning only to find that Jenny, the woman he loves had left him, and his solution was to run.

Unlike the main character in the movie, I didn't put on my running shoes. I calmly walked out of the doctor's office, got into the car with my mother and spoke no word until I closed my bedroom door. After collapsing on the floor next to my bed I cursed God. "Darn you! Darn you for creating me! Darn You!" The pain and tears were uncontainable. "I hate you!" I shouted towards the ceiling. "I hate you, I hate your Church and I hate everything. I've ever heard about you."

For the next several days, I secretly stopped taking my prescribed medication. I refused to go to school and refused to leave my bedroom. All day and all night, I starred at the ceiling reflecting on my life: "I'm 13. I have no friends, no joy, no peace, and no future." I needed a jump-start to a new life. For a moment, I thought about packing a suitcase and running away. I desperately wanted to escape but had no options and no real chance of success.

I knew where my brother hid alcohol. I saw it the previous week while I was walking through the woods behind our house. After several minutes of considering how I could steal it, bring it in my bedroom, drink it, and not get caught, I devised my plan. It was almost 5 o'clock and my father would arrive home from work soon. I had no time to spare.

Carefully I pretended to take my dog, Lightning, for a walk. After wearing extra baggy pants and a sweater, I put the leash on Lightning and calmly walked down the street towards Potters Hill. Discreetly I glanced around to see if anyone was watching, and when everything was clear Lighting and I ran as fast as we could into the woods.

"We made it! No one saw us girl," I quietly said to Lightning. She and I had been best friends ever since my family got her as a puppy. After several minutes of kicking around through the leaves and turning over some rotted wood I finally found it. The two 40oz bottles of Busch Light was now within my grasp.

Apart from the taste of wine at Sunday Church service, I had never really tasted alcohol before. I was full of both fear and excitement, and for some strange reason I felt immense pleasure from the thought of doing something illegal.

After looking around to make sure no one spotted me, I discreetly stuffed the two dirty bottles into my pants and covered the bulge with my oversized sweater. It became hard to walk normally while concealing the bottles. Now, as I look back, I can see the symbolism of that four block walk back to my house. It was the same juggling act I had faced day after day.

I felt my heart pounding harder and harder in my chest, the closer I got to home. Thoughts of hiding the bottles somewhere or running away entered my mind but I was determined. I didn't even consider that I was stealing from my brother or what this weak moral choice could lead to; I just wanted it. I didn't know why I wanted it, but I desperately craved it.

As I finally reached my parents driveway with Lightning's leash in one hand and the bottles of beer being held with my other, my heart stopped. I saw my father's van parked outside the house, he was home already. My perfect plan had reached a fatal flaw. I had to decide either to continue on with the plan and risk being caught or try to ditch the evidence somewhere in the street and hope no one saw me.

Without deviating from my plan, I soon learned something about myself. I could hide the fear within me if I focused on the end goal. I put Lightning in her kennel, opened the front door to our two story house, said hello to my father, smiled, and walked upstairs to my bedroom arising no suspicions.

However, the moment I closed my bedroom door, the adrenaline I was feeling was quickly replaced with anxiety. I quickly hid the alcohol, ran to my bed, got in and pulled the blankets over my head until I felt myself calm down. I was only halfway finished with my overall plan. I only obtained the substance; I still needed to consume it without getting caught.

That night, my father made lasagna for dinner. I always enjoyed my father's cooking and tonight's meal was one of my favorites. Throughout the entire meal, no one suspected anything. No one had a clue what I brought into our home merely an hour before. I engaged in conversation and my parents even commented on the positive attitude I expressed that night. Little did they know the reason for my mood, but they were excited that their son was smiling again and for that they were thankful.

After dinner and everyone went to sleep, I opened the drawer I hid the bottles in earlier that evening. It was 11:37 p.m. Raising the bottle to my lips, I tasted the beer the minute the warm liquid touched my tongue. It was disgusting!

Even though the taste was horrible, the effects were still the same. The more I drank, the faster my fears mysteriously slipped away. I forgot about my childhood trauma, I forgot about my depression. I even forgot that I had no friends. That night I slept better and more peacefully than all my nights before. It's safe to say I enjoyed my first drink.

That next morning, I carefully protected my new hobby from being exposed. I gently placed the empty bottles in my backpack and walked to school. While walking to school I tossed the empty bottles in an empty lot where no one would see. I will never forget the feeling I had in class that day. I was proud. I wasn't proud of my life but I was proud because my plan succeeded and I got away with it! I had started my new life.

It wasn't long after I found other people in my school that enjoyed alcohol as much as I did. For the first time in my life, I found friends. These people wanted to be near me, not because they could make jokes about me or about my weight, but because we enjoyed the same hobby — Alcohol.

My newfound friends and I would get together whenever we could. My family noticed a change in my life. My clothes changed, my attitude changed, and my entire focus changed. Before I would never want to leave the house; now I never wanted to stay in the house. Eventually, I was away from my parents' home so much that they never truly knew what I was doing or who I was with.

Some of the changes I enjoyed were: my new friends, the freedom, and the intensity of life, but the negative changes were quickly and quietly gaining momentum. I reasoned with myself until I lived in a world full of compromise. I thought it was normal to consume alcohol every weekend. I suffered through each weekday just so I can have the sweet release on the weekends.

By the time High School began, I noticed my friends and I were drifting away. They were focused on football and other school activities, while I was more focused on self-medicating. To stay connected I got involved as much as I could with school activities. I spent over 12 hours each day on campus, while also working at the local grocery store, part-time, to earn money.

Between lifting weights, football practice, high school plays, choir and band, I was a very involved student. On the surface level, unless you knew me, you would assume nothing was wrong; but inside, I was consumed with pain, desperately trying to be normal and accepted.

The night of our first high school dance, my secret would be exposed. At the request of my friends, we left the dance early. Though we were already drunk from the vodka we consumed in the school bathroom, we decided we needed more, and what better place to get it then a private party. Together, we raced in our separate cars trying to see who would be the first one to the party.

I can still remember the look on Mike's face as he slammed on his breaks, trying to avoid the oncoming car. For a moment, it seemed as though time moved in slow motion as we crashed into the SUV. We hit SUV so hard the oncoming car flipped twice in the air before rolling down the hill and finally coming to a stop. Thankfully, the air bags release just moments before my head smashed into the reinforced glass window.

With the help of the police, I slowly got out of wrecked car, relieved to hear no one was killed. Both cars were destroyed but miraculously no one involved sustained fatal injuries. As soon as the police discovered alcohol was involved, we could no longer hide our secret. All of us involved were sentenced to complete our first substance abuse program.

The program was as fast as it was easy, and with the encouragement of my 'friends', I tried to stay out of the spotlight as much as possible. I could no longer drink at the house because my parents knew I had a problem. Besides, the effects and smell of alcohol were too easy to spot,

I needed to self-medicate, but my resources were now extremely limited.

Nearly a month after all the drama from the accident subsided, things slowly returned to normal. It felt great to spend my weekends drinking with my friends again. I was going to more and more parties and meeting many strange, yet interesting people.

Two weeks before my first high school play, my friend Brice had a surprise for me. I had never seen it before and didn't really understand what it was or how to use it. I had only seen it in the movies and thought I could gain a lot of money selling it. My part-time job at the local grocery store wasn't enough to cover my drinking habit, so I was always looking for ways to generate extra income.

"How much is it?" I asked.

"$120." Brice replied.

My first thought was "how can I ever afford this?" Still there was something mysterious and mesmerizing about it. I just couldn't look away. Without any hesitation, I made the purchase to buy something that would enhance my life, I thought. I believed I was investing in my future and honestly thought it was a smart decision. I walked away from that bathroom stall feeling confident and found myself heading towards my morning history class without a care in the world.

Brice had promised to give me a ride home from football practice, so that same night we met in the school parking lot. We took a detour down an old dusty road like we had many times before. Normally we did this to drink beers, or smoke cigarettes, but this night was different. This night Brice and I had other plans.

As he stopped the car in our normal place, I heard Brice ask, "Do you have what I sold you?"

"Of course" I replied.

"Good, let me see it. I'll show you how to use it." As Brice opened the bag, the smell consumed the car like strong potpourri. He took out his bronze pipe and compacted it full of this enticing substance. As he brought the pipe to his lips, he lit the bowl with a lighter, sucking in the flavor that even to this day is difficult to describe.

"Let's hotbox this thing," he stated with a smirk, as he exhaled the smoke in our already stuffy car.

As he handed me the loaded pipe and lighter I had an instant of awareness about my decision. Everything about this night differed completely from every night before. I was making a bad decision, a decision that would alter the rest of my existence.

Glancing at the pipe once again, then glaring at Brice I laughed almost nervously as I joked, "Well, soon I will become a hopeless drug addict living on the streets with a needle hanging out of my arm right?"

As I heard Brice laugh, I knew this wasn't so much a joke as it was a possibility. Placing the pipe against my lips, I flicked the lighter, and took the plunge inhaling my first puff of Marijuana.

"Who has woe? Who has sorrow? Who has strife? Who has complaints? Who has needle bruises? Who has bloodshot eyes? Those who linger over wine, who go to sample bowls of mixed wine. Do not gaze at wine when it is red, when it sparkles in the cup, when it goes down smoothly! In the end it bites like a snake and poisons like viper. Your eyes will see strange sights and your mind imagine confusing things. You will be like one sleeping on the high seas, lying on top of the rigging. 'They hit me,' you

will say, 'but I'm not hurt! They beat me, but I don't feel it! When will I wake up so I can find another drink?'"

- **Proverbs 23:29-35**

CHAPTER THREE:

A Living Hell

September 11, 2002
8:39 a.m.

R. BUSCHER, YOU MAY REMAIN SILENT. Anything you do or say can be used against you in the court of law. You have the right to an attorney. If you can't afford an attorney, one will be appointed to you. Do you understand your rights?" The officer read me my Miranda rights as the deputies were placing the shackles on my wrists and ankles.

I didn't respond. I couldn't. I was in complete shock – at 16-years-old, already being dragged away as if I was type of dangerous animal. My mother was trying to hold herself together as my father removed my sisters from the scene. I'll admit, the arrest was warranted; but the show of force was for humiliation only.

One month prior, my family's home was raided and my mini drug "ring" was taken down. Having spent the last two years selling Marijuana and prescription narcotics, I was now placed on house arrest while awaiting trial. The terms of my release were simple: attend daily therapy for substance abuse, stay sober, and attend school. However, having been expelled within days of starting my junior year, I was now in direct violation and subject to re-arrest.

This couldn't have come at a worse time. All my money was on the street. I had no warning and couldn't prepare monetarily for the situation I now found myself in. Everything was now lost and I possessed only the clothes on my back. As the police placed me in back seat of the impala, I remembered my mother's face. Her expression represented the shame I had placed on her and the family. She would now have to go to her job as a respected nurse, only to face the ridicule of people knowing what happened to her son.

The next three hours I was silent. I watched the rain fall down on the car's window as the officers sped down the highway. They wouldn't tell me where they were taking me and I didn't ask. All I could do was tremble in fear as I regretted every decision I had made that put me here.

28

From a distance, I could see the watch towers and barbed wire fence encompassing the grey fortress. I wanted to cry. I wanted to beg for mercy. I wanted my situation to be different. Knowing the officers were watching my reactions in the rearview mirror, I tried to appear calm and strong. Surely my survival depended on these initial moments. Even if I wanted to shed a tear I couldn't. I haven't been able to cry in years so why should today be any different?

The senior officer opened my door then tugged forcefully on my chain signaling me to move forward. As I began my walk of shame up the path that led to the prison walls, I refused to look back. It was time to accept what I was and adapt to my new surroundings. It was time to become inmate number 70755134.

The first moments of prison are the worst. They take away your name and replace it with a number. They remove your clothes and shoes and replaced them with a colored uniform and sandals.You are then escorted to a 5 x 8 cell, which becomes your home for the duration of your stay. The amenities were practically non-existent: No television, no phone, and no photos. You're only allowed a Bible, a worn out set of sheets, and a pillow.

The first several hours I was alone. I didn't know it but I was in a transitional cell while awaiting the local government to finish processing my paperwork. Everything happened so fast I didn't have time to process it all. I heard the screams coming from down the hall. They sounded so horrific that my blood chilled and I quit breathing. All I could think was, "How could this be happening to me? I'm only 16."

As the sun set in the sky, I tried to pretend I was anywhere but there, while desperately trying to reassure myself this was only temporary. Without warning, my cell door opened.

"Stand-up," said one of the guards, with an angry expression on his face. "Don't look at me, look at the floor."

Before I could respond, his club was thrust into my stomach and I was dragged out of my cell and pushed into another.

I couldn't open my eyes. I didn't want them to see the fear controlling me at this moment. As the cell door slammed shut, I slowly opened my eyes catching the first glimpse of my cell mate, Demarco.

Demarco and I were from separate worlds. He was from the inner city and I was from a small Midwestern community. He was facing many years for his crimes, while I would be released at 18. Demarco was known for his violence in and out of his cell, while I was new and all alone.

I wasn't strong enough when he attacked me. I wasn't prepared. The first night, after the lights shut off, Demarco made his move. While forcing his hands over my mouth, he pressed a sharp object to my throat.

"Keep your mouth shut," he said in a harsh whisper.

As I fought him off I felt something pierce my chest. My muscles refused to function as I passed out lying covered in my own blood. The guards must have heard the commotion because when I awoke I was being stitched up in the prison medical room.

After my first night in the infirmary, I was placed in solitary confinement. Twenty four hours a day, seven days a week, all alone in my cell. Even with a Bible less than an arm's reach away, I still refused to acknowledge the book. I refused to read it even if only for entertainment.

When my father and mother first came to visit, all I could do was cry. I couldn't tell them what had happened, they wouldn't have understood. They would have only made my situation worse. I could only repeat "Please, get me out of here. Please. Please, I beg you get me out of here."

After two months my attorney could finally schedule a transfer to another city. It was a lower level facility where I would be given the opportunity to serve my time, while continuing my education and receiving rigorous around the clock substance abuse therapy.

I thrived in this new facility. It differed completely from the other. I was given an opportunity and I fully intended on staying there. My attorney warned me if there were any incidents, I would be returned to the previous facility for the maximum sentence allowed.

The first two months, I kept my mouth shut and my head down. I watched and I waited. I spoke the right words, showed the right emotions, and strategically became a trusted resident in the facility. I made sure my good deeds were known, not only to the staff, but to my family. No one saw my next moves coming.

During the Christmas season, my family could have an unsupervised visit with me. It was the opportunity I was waiting for. For the last month I had been testing the limitations of security of the facility and felt comfortable with the newly devised plan of escape. Using my father's cell phone, without his knowledge, I could communicate a pickup location date and time for transportation. Everything was organized and waiting for my follow-through.

December 27, 2002

Waking up a few minutes early to neatly arrange the sheets on my bed, I gazed into the mirror and smiled thinking: "it's game time". I brushed my teeth in the individual sink and calmly strutted down the hall the same as any other day. The cameras were always watching and even the slightest hesitation or quickening of my pace could alert the staff something was strange was going on.

All throughout the day, I needed to be extra careful. Even through educational and meal times, I needed to be on my guard. Even the smallest alteration in the daily schedule could affect my plan of escape. After the last meal of the day, quiet hours would begin. During quiet hours the staff administered bed checks every 35 minutes by shining a flashlight to see our physical bodies and to confirm our presence in the facility, as required by state and federal law.

I could hear the night guard quietly making his rounds down each hall. From previous watches, this meant the time was precisely 10:05 p.m. Nearly 2 miles away, in an abandoned farm, a black Cutlass would wait for my arrival at exactly 11:30pm. If I was late or police were spotted, the Cutlass was instructed to abandon the pickup and leave the scene. This was my only opportunity of escape. Everything had to be exact, everything had to be perfect. If I would be apprehended, 5 years would be added to my sentence for attempting to escape. It's safe to say I had reason to be on edge that night.

At 10:07 p.m., the light shone through my door and my flash of skin was accepted as the guard passed along to the next room. Slowly I slid down my mattress onto the floor. I needed to remove money I had tucked away over the last several months here. It was not a fortune, but it was enough for the passage to freedom. After quietly retrieving the money, I dressed in the warmest clothes I could. I quickly returned to my mattress before the next bed check.

At 10:40 p.m., the guard was early. I didn't have enough time to slow my breath causing the guard to suspiciously shine the light around the room. He's looking for something, anything to give him reason to open the door and toss my room. Thirty seconds have passed and he's still watching

"Stop breathing so hard" I ordered myself, "Calm down or else."

By some miracle, the pillar of light from his flashlight passed by as he went on to the next room. I needed to wait an additional 5 minutes for the guard to clear the hall, so he would be far enough not to hear the sound that came next.

At 10:47 p. M., I used the sheets to wrap some supplies for my journey. Inside I placed extra clothes, money and a homemade weapon and I threw it over my shoulder as I quietly crept towards the window. I am over 3 meters above the ground and there was less than 40 minutes until my window of opportunity closed. I had no choice, no other options. It was now or never. As fast as I could, I placed the sheets on my chest, covered my head, and then violently dove through the glass window towards the inescapable darkness.

Crashing hard onto the ground I felt pain radiate throughout my body. I wanted to just lay there and surrender, but as the motion alarms sounded and the lights turned on, I knew I had to keep moving. My heart was pounding in my chest and I could feel the adrenaline surging through my veins. I jolted to my feet, but my left foot wouldn't move.

"I must have sprained it on the crash landing," I thought as I ran as fast as I could towards the shadows projecting out from a tree in the moonlight.

Finally I made it to the barn and I could see the dim glow from the glass on the Cutlass waiting for my arrival.

"I'm not too late," I thought as I gasped for air.

Hobbling along the frozen winter ground, I saw flashes of the red and blue police lights in the distance as the man in the car signaled for me to move faster fearing for his own safety.

"Where are they? Get in the trunk," he shouted.

"There is no one following me yet, but they can't be too far behind," I replied.

As the trunk shut, the car discreetly drove away. The irony of my situation didn't escape me. I exchanged one cell for another tonight. My new cell was the trunk of a car trying to put as much distance between itself and the facility from which I had escaped. The difference was this cell was a familiar one and belonged to my best friend. At that moment, I knew where I was going. I was going back to the streets.

As the sun climbed in the morning sky, I could see the rays of light enter through the small cracks of the cars imperfect structure. We had been driving all night and it was now almost time to stop for fuel. At this point we were far enough away I could leave the trunk and sit in the car with my friend. As the car came to a stop, I heard the trunk open and saw his familiar face.

"Jack, my most loyal friend, how the heck are you?" I asked excitedly.

We hadn't spoken a word all night. I was relieved to embrace my friend and smell the fresh air on the old abandoned road. Getting into the car I noticed a care package waiting for me under my seat: cigarettes, beer, and a small assortment of narcotics. This was my salvation, the reason I had escaped.

Within minutes of enjoying the assortment, all my pain and fear once again left me. I was enjoying the open road and had every intention of staying hidden. I was now a wanted man and anyone caught with me could be convicted of aiding and harboring a fugitive. I could not contact friends or family without putting them at risk. Even if I wanted to, they would most likely try to convince me to turn myself in. They would rather see me in a prison cell than see me die on the streets from the narcotics I was indulging in.

As all things in life, nothing lasts forever. As a 16-year-old boy, wanted by the authorities, high on narcotics, and running out of money, I was running fast towards destruction. After only 4 days of abusing my body with every chemical imaginable, karma finally caught up with me. I tried opiates for the first time and I took one too many. My first official drug overdose was in the backseat of that car on Highway 18 going West bound.

Fearing for my life, my friend Jack gave me over to the authorities for medical treatment where I was then safely returned to the Lower Level Facility. To this day, I don't understand how my attorney swindled the judge into allowing me to return there instead of sentencing me to maximum security. Either way, one thing

was for sure, I was given another opportunity —
an opportunity I didn't deserve but one for which
I was grateful.

On my return to the facility, I remained bed
ridden for the first several days. Thankfully I was
given time to regain my strength before facing
my peers. This time, the separation from others
left me in a state of complete solitude. It was
probably the best technique they ever used. I
could reflect on my life and my choices with no
interruption. They continuously informed me I
was only here for a probation period. The courts
still were debating on where to permanently
place me. I knew that if I wanted to remain there
and not be returned to prison, I had to prove
myself quickly.

At first I was angry and I didn't enjoy being
locked away, but part of me knew I needed help.
I didn't want to be a criminal or a drug addict.
All I ever wanted was to be accepted and normal.
I had made so many decisions based off
selfishness and greed and now all I wanted was
help, I just didn't know how to get it.

I thought about a man who worked at this
facility. Dave, or Pastor as some called him, was
a Christian man. He always seemed full of joy
and treated us differently than the others. He

tried to bring hope when all many of us saw was darkness. Until that moment, I had always rejected his help, but tonight of all nights I couldn't stop thinking about him.

I had a dream that night. I saw all of my friends and business associates surrounding me. They violently tied me to a stake and beat me. They called me a traitor and spat on my face. One man pulled hairs from my head as he laughed devilishly—the laugh that expresses immense joy and satisfaction in someone else's pain.

"Darkness is coming, Darkness is coming," an old woman whispered in my ear as she stabbed my kidney with a spike.

The moment the spike pierced my flesh I found myself once again lying in my bed trembling.

"It's only a dream, it's only a dream," I said over and over as a mantra.

Attempting to stand to my feet I realized something was wrong. I couldn't move. Neither my arms nor my legs. My first reaction was to cry out for help, but my voice wouldn't work. I felt as if I was paralyzed and I was. I was overcome with fear. I had allowed fear to control my thoughts for so long; it now paralyzed my physical body and refused to release me.

While stuck in the state of panic, all I could think about was Pastor Dave. I couldn't speak, I couldn't move, I could only think. The moment I attempted to speak a word for help, only one word escaped mouth "JESUS". As soon as the word left my lips, I felt my arms and legs come free.

Awaking from the dream the next morning, I felt like a changed man. That small dream gave me the strength I needed to give the facility a real chance. I listened to my instructors and excelled in the tasks they assigned. After 8 months of diligent progress, the courts gave me my freedom. My attorney even convinced the courts to seal my record, starting at 18, so my future wouldn't be judged by my past mistakes as a juvenile. I was now 17-years-old standing at the exit with a High School Diploma, free, with the opportunity to start a new life.

"As a dog returns to its vomit, so a fool repeats his folly"

- **Proverbs 26:11**

CHAPTER FOUR:

I Can Make It on My Own

WELCOME HOME CHRIS," my younger sister Anne said apprehensively. She hadn't seen me in months and the brother that left had been a monster.

"Mom, Sadie and I are going outside to play," she said as she and her friend hurried out the door. I could understand why she still feared me. The last time she saw me, I was holding a butchers knife to her wrist, threatening to remove her hand.

I wanted to change, I really did. All that filled me was the desire to do my best, yet I knew something was missing from my twisted life. On the outside I was clean and sober, but on the inside I was still lost and full of shame. Like a beach ball held under water, it was only a matter of time before it burst up and shot up into the air. I was a ticking time bomb, ready to explode in a moment's notice.

Within days of trying unsuccessfully to withhold my feelings, I packed a bag and leave my family's home.

"I put them through enough," I thought as I remorsefully organized my belongings. "I can make it on my own," I said to my mother as she attempted to convince me to stay.

"You're only 17, you have no money, and you were only recently released from state lockup. Where do you think you will go?" my desperate mom inquired.

I can't even imagine her pain as I kissed her on the cheek and left the house that Wednesday afternoon. She was right; I had nothing, no prospective opportunities awaiting me. My only comfort was that I knew that I was doing the right thing by not letting my family see my self-destructive behavior.

I spent the last $20 I had on a carton of cigarettes, a half-gallon of vodka, and started down the road towards hopelessness. My only currency was now manipulation and for me, manipulation was a tool I has mastered on the streets. I could get what I wanted from people before they knew they were being conned.

I slept on the sofa in a dealer's house while working for him to pay for my drug habits. The drug he was peddling didn't come from Mexico or any other foreign country, he manufactured it himself. This new powder substance was as profitable as it was destructive. Having been made mostly from local household chemicals, it was relatively inexpensive to create, yet sometimes sold at prices higher than the cocaine on the street.

"It expensive because of the risks involved," he explained. "One wrong step, one wrong addition to the recipe, and the house will burst in flames. "Trusting the wrong person will put all of us in prison for 50 years," Brian warned me. He taught me a skill that helped me survive years on the street; he taught me how to successfully cook Crystal Meth.

From the first time I tasted meth, the feeling of poisonous chemicals overpowered me. If it wasn't for the immediate feeling that followed, I would have vomited. Before this moment, I tried every drug imaginable, but nothing compared to grip Meth instantly held over me. Every use sent waves of energetic pleasures through every part of my body. It seemed as if I thought more clearly, accomplished more, and curbed my appetite.

Within weeks of daily use, I stopped sleeping and discontinued eating almost entirely. Rapid weight loss and tooth decay set in as the smell of my sweat changed to the odor of cat urine. I could feel nothing and was too afraid to see my reflection in the mirror. I lived only for my next fix.

With a drug habit of over $200 a day, you quickly learn to kill your conscience before your conscience kills you. Without remorse, I stole from everyone and took anything that appeared valuable. It didn't matter how big or small, I stole it. The need to feed the needle into my arm was the only thing I lived for. With every violent act and every gram drained into my veins, I forgot who I was and had no idea what I had become.

It wasn't long before the police would quit playing 'catch and release' with me. Having been known in different communities for my crimes, it was now a high priority for the local police to put me away for good. They had grown tired of my habitual offenses and were biding their time to create their case.

"Wake up! Wake up!" I heard as my body was being shaken.

"Joey, what the heck do you want?" I replied.

"I need your help. Grab some bags, some tools, and follow me," he said.

I didn't know what was happening. I had just crashed from a 14 day bender without sleep and I refused to arise from my slumber.

Apparently, he had found a safe during a drunken fit of vandalism and thievery, thought its contents would help us purchase our next fix. After continuously refusing to assist in this robbery he went on ahead without me. I had been with him many times before and have done much worse myself, but tonight was just one of those nights I was too tired.

Waking up the next morning, I found myself full of anger when I saw our house. We had destroyed it with the months of partying and our lack of effort spent cleaning our once beautiful home. Garbage, broken bottles, empty bags, and dirty needles were everywhere. We lived in your typical drug den surrounded by many comatose junkies. I was not surprised by this, after all I was used to it. I was angered, angered that my brother had done something so careless.

I found him passed out in the basement cellar covered in mud and surrounded by piles of evidence from what he did.

"Joey, what is your problem? Where were you? What did you do?" I yelled as I grabbed him and violently tossed him around.

He didn't need to answer, somehow I already knew. Before he even spoke the words, I knew we were all about to be to be arrested. It was only a matter of time.

As quickly as I could I destroyed the evidence. I needed to be fast and efficient before the doors would be kicked in and all of us taken out. After shoveling everything into large black plastic bags, I drove them out of the city limits. Having done this same ritual several times before over the years, it had become second nature.

After getting back to the house, I made everyone leave that wasn't involved. The last thing we needed was more witnesses. We tried to create a solid alibi; one that the police wouldn't be able to solve. Finally, after going around in circles, we decided we could think better if we were high.

While we were leaving the house to purchase our treasured crystal meth, something out of the corner of my eye caught my attention. By the time I realized what it was, it was already too late. The police had barricaded my car in the driveway and silently surrounded the house.

"Exit the vehicle and place your hands where I can see them. DO IT NOW!" the officer shouted from behind me.

Pausing for a moment, I knew I was out of options. Any hesitation or compulsive decision on my part could cause gun fire. Watching the police drag my brother out of the house, I understood it was time to surrender. While shoving me on the hood of the car, a needle fell out of my pocket, which is when they then searched me. Eventually the officers found enough narcotics and weapons to give me a minimum of five years in prison. They watched me, they wanted me, and now they finally had me.

Once again I would hear the words; "You have the right to remain silent, anything you do or say can be used against you in the court of law." Hearing my rights read to me as the restraints were placed on my wrists helped to put my life in perspective. I was lost, and my life was

48

over. Anger and resentment were suppressed by the meth I had ingested only moments before, but deep down I knew they would soon emerge.

The officers escorted me to the police station where they seated me in a chair with blue felt. I had sat there numerous times before. While in these chairs, you're treated like less than nothing. The temperature is cold and you're served nothing to drink while you await the inquisition. During moments such as this, my mind raced: how can I spin the truth, how can I escape, how can I not go back to prison?

"Mr. Buscher, my name is Officer Kyle Banks. Do you understand the charges against you," he asked as if I could forget his name. I remember his name. He has been my arresting officer 12 times now in the last 3 years.

"How high do you think I am Banks?" I responded sarcastically. "Let's just get this over with," I continued on.

As minutes quickly turned into hours it became apparent what they wanted. They had been threatening me and creating visions of a failed future. With all of this hopelessness in the air, Officer Jeb Fetch piped up.

"There is a way out of this Mr. Buscher, we know you weren't there. Other witnesses say you tried to avoid this situation; that you were even angry it happened. All we need from you is to confirm the testimony of the collaborating witness and you are free to go home."

Despite how high I was at that moment, I understood what they were asking. They wanted me to decide: Serve another five years for the narcotics plus added felonies for helping hide my brother's crimes, or surrender my brother and be set free the same day. I couldn't speak and was lost in a daze of confinement. I knew my decision here on this day would affect the rest of my life no matter what I chose.

"We will give you a moment to think about your future, if you even want one," said Fetch, as he and Banks left me alone with my thoughts.

Paralyzed by those thoughts, I was drifting in and out of consciousness. It had now been several hours since my last fix and the meth was taking its physical toll on me. I entered the crash phase of the meth train and I knew if I didn't get a fix soon, the pain and discomfort would become the least of my worries.

As I was nodding off, the metal door of the interrogation room suddenly opened. Officer Banks was accompanied by two other men. One of the men I recognized as Officer Fetch, but the bald man wearing a cheap suit I hadn't seen before. One look at this man and it was clear he was just as slimy as the god awful cologne he bathed in. As he arrogantly walked over to the table, I couldn't help but notice that everything about him pointed to dramatic overcompensation for his pathetic existence.

"My name is not important, what is important is that you sign your name to these documents in my hand." He stated.

As I glanced through the documents I understood even without my testimony they had a pile of evidence against us.

"How could they have gathered such details so quickly?" I thought as my hands shook relentlessly.

As sweat began to roll off my face, my head nodded as I reached for the pen. This was the moment of weakness they were waiting for. I signed my name and gave them exactly what they wanted. Through this coercion, I delivered them my brother.

Leaving the police station, I thought I would be free just like they promised. I thought I could return to my home, put a needle in my arm, and forget today ever happened. I was wrong. From the moment they door closed and released me onto the street I was completely overwhelmed by a cloud of guilt and shame.

I made no telephone calls or inform anyone I was released. I took another way to my home to go unnoticed. Parking my car two blocks away I quietly crept through the rear entrance of our dark home. Not having turned on the lights, I felt my way to the basement. There alone in the dark I allowed myself to finally feel the pain.

I cried loudly and uncontrollably. The weight hit me like a ton of bricks falling from the sky. "This wasn't the freedom I was promised! What type of animal would rat on his own brother! I should be in a cell with him, but instead I am here hiding in this damp basement alone and afraid." The words came through my tears as if someone was saying my confession. Instinctively I crawled on my hands and knees to my secret hiding place were my needles were stored. As I prepared to inject myself with more of the poison destroying my life, I remorsefully uttered: "It's just you and me now. I have given you everything. Now I understand the pains of addiction. Damn you Crystal Meth..."

"The thief comes to steal, kill, and destroy... He is a Liar and the Father of lies..."

- **John 10:10; 8:44**

CHAPTER FIVE:

Beyond All Hope

December 18, 2005

A RE YOU SURE THIS WILL WORK?" said Biggy. "Why do we need to take so many? I'm not sure about this Chris," Justin said to support Biggy's doubts.

Justin and Biggy were a pair of lost souls following me on my path to Hell. Over the last few years, we had known each other and more recently lived together to support each other's drug habits.

"Shut up and trust me," I said, taking command of the group as I swallowed my pills. It was their first experience with this medication, but it wasn't mine. I was introduced to DXM many years ago while trying to get high on a tight budget. DXM is an illegal narcotic, but it can found in many cough suppressant medications. The effects were similar to my experiences with heroin and acid. However this wasn't my reason for the consumption of the large quantities.

Weeks before this day, I had read a study on the effects of the medication containing the desired DXM. The report said that constant abuse often led to literal holes developing in the brain contributing to permanent memory loss. More side effects included organ shutdown, kidney failure, and ultimately death. For a man whose shadow was covered in constant regret of his past mistakes, this seemed like the perfect opportunity to forget everything once and for all.

At 11:32 a.m., the three of us formed our circle and swallowed the medication. To receive the desired effects we needed to each consume 16 pills. For those inexperienced to drug addiction, most people would have second thoughts before consuming so many. However we knew what we were; we weren't business men in suits, or honest hard working citizens. We were drug addicts and we proudly called ourselves professional drug addicts.

After swallowing the pills, we relaxed on the floor sipping on warm beer from the previous night's debauchery. As the minutes passed by, I could see the doubt forming in their eyes and the sweat dripping from their palms as they nervously brushed them against their filthy clothes. We were in an unstable existence waiting for the prime opportunity to collapse.

As my stomach rumbled, my sweat dripped more grease from my pimpled face. It felt as if I was locked in a blazing furnace with an endless supply of fuel. With the rise of my body temperature, my eye sight failed. Suddenly I felt the need to vomit and crawled to the toilet as to not create a scene. Before my mouth even opened the acids hurled out of my decaying jaws and onto the rotting floor. I had never vomited so much in my life and with such force. Though the pain was intense, with each release, my body temperature seemed to cool and at that moment the pressure released.

I laid there covered in my own disgust and drenched by my bodily fluids. In that small studio apartment, we all found something. Though the experience was unique to each, the three of us spent the next 12 hours in an altered state of existence, entirely captivated by our own personal fantasy world. I didn't know who I was or what I was doing. I had successfully become numb to my past, present, and future. I found the keys to the spiritual door I desperately wanted opened and I entered the room at full speed.

As the hours passed, my existence in the world I had left now slowly returned. With each minute, I regained my strength and soon I knew I could walk again. Having contemplated whether to leave my comrades and venture out into the streets in search of more pills, I thought it best to wait for their recovery hoping they would join me. It was unanimous, I didn't need to ask, they wanted it as much as I needed it.

Nervously I reached for the gold wristwatch my grandfather had given me. It was my only possession left in this world.

"Its 11:15pm," I shouted. "Get up! Let's go! Hurry before the store closes," I continued.

To get more pills, the three of us raced down the street still under the influence of strong narcotics.

"How is Justin? Will he be able to drive? I can barely walk." I reasoned but soon my thoughts redirected themselves towards the goal of another dose.

After many more moments of blackouts and near fatal collisions, we finally arrived at our destination. Kicking open the door of the rusted out Chevy impala, I stepped towards the goal as a champion seeing his victory before his eyes. The moment my foot touched the ground, my full body weight followed. My legs were so weak I couldn't support myself and my body tumbled onto the ground.

"Get up! Hurry Chris," said Biggy as he and Justin grabbed my arms to help stabilize me.

It seemed like hours trying to reach the automatic doors of Walmart but, in all reality, it was only a matter of minutes. We were stumbling and having the robotic motion of zombies mesmerized by the anticipation of consuming more and more. I'm sure we looked like something straight out of the movies. I don't know why the police weren't called or why the employees continued to sell us the medication. But as I held the boxes of medication in my hands, strength came upon me and with all the grace and stability of a solider marching in, we uniformly returned to our car ready to consume our spoils.

Climbing back into the car was no easy task.

"Ouch! That would hurt if I could feel anything," I thought as I hit my head and arms on different parts of the car while maneuvering my way through the seats and random garbage from months without care.

"Justin, you got Mustard on my jeans, how about you clean your car!" I said, repulsed by the situation I was climbing into. No matter how disgusted I was by the way we lived, life without drugs forced me to accept the conditions of others.

"Let me see them," I demanded. Proudly, Justin and Biggy revealed what they were doing while I distracted the employees by purchasing four boxes of Coricidin. Within the next five minutes they removed 22 boxes they concealed in their pants. We now had 26 boxes, or 416 DXM pills.

"Each one of us could get high another eight times," I said as I sensed the feeling of relief filling the car. Sharing a warm beer we washed the pills down and return to the safety of Justin's studio apartments like rats hiding from the storm.

We spent the whole day barricaded in the apartment tripping on pills while our minds slowly left us. After the third 12 hour trip into the world of DXM, we had each forgotten what reality was. We had become slaves to this new drug and continually attempted to push our limits to the next level. The pills we stole should have lasted us days but they didn't. We needed more and more to reach the desired effects.

Our tolerance had jumped from 16 to 32 pills every 12 hours and our stash was dangerously depleted. It's almost unimaginable how strange we had become in the last 36 hours since venturing out into the society. Dehydrated with sunken faces and disorientated limps, we stomped in the only motion DXM would allowed us. We saw everything different, nothing was the same. Nothing mattered except the prospect of more DXM.

From what was once a 3 minute walk from the upstairs apartment to Justin's car now became a 1 hour obstacle. With determination, we attempted to stick the key inside the ignition, but even with the collaborated assistance of each of us this seemed to be an impossible task. With a brief moment, a clarity we understood was that we could no longer operate any motorized vehicle, let alone be trusted to safely walk anywhere without assistance.

Sitting in that car, in the freezing cold with mountains of snow and ice surrounding us, a friend spotted us from a distance.

"Where the heck have you been?" Kayla said while attempting to open the passenger door. Kayla had known us for years but she never fully grasped the full extent of our drug addiction. Maybe it's because she herself occasionally drank alcohol and experimented with mild narcotics.

Slurring my words I replied, "I don't know where we have been but I now where we are going."

After demanding we leave the car and go with her, we agreed on the pretense she would help us. She didn't understand why we wanted to go to the store or what we were attempting to accomplish. She was a friend merely attempting to save us from our own destruction while naively believing if she became our baby sitter, we wouldn't kill ourselves or someone else in a car accident. With her assistance, she became our chauffeur and together we left the parking lot on a mission.

We had no money and could barely walk, but never underestimate the desperation of drug addicts with nothing left to loose. Within one hour of the apartment, we were once holed up in another city with several stores that sold the medication we needed. We started on the north side of the city and worked our way to the very southern tip, stopping at every store along the way. We ventured from the obvious box stores like Walmart and Target, all the way to your little grocery stores and 24-hour pharmacies. To avoid easy detection, we removed the pills from the boxes before leaving each store. Not able to purchase a single item, we strolled into the stores focused on our mission, quickly exiting after 5 minutes. We stuffed our pants with the medication as we left a line of boxes throughout each isle of the unsuspecting stores.

By the end of the day, there were no more stores to enter and our bodies craved the medication. Unless the store owners had reservation boxes hidden in their building, we left a city of 50,000 people completely without Coricidin.

It was now 10:03 p.m. and Kayla wanted to bring us home. She still did not understand what she had just a part been of. After delivering us to Justin's apartment building, I attempted to leave the car with the large black garbage bag. Since I could not carry the bag and myself up the stairs, Kayla assisted me.

The moment Justin's apartment door opened we all collapsed on the floor joyfully clinging to the mysterious black garbage bag.

"What heck is in that bag?" Kayla demanded.

"It's none of your business! Don't worry about it, it's nothing," we retorted.

Angrily she ripped part of the plastic from our fingers as thousands of pills spilled onto the floor.

"Oh my God! Oh my God! What have you guys done?" She asked as we could literally seethe fear in her eyes.

Like chickens pecking for their food, we gathered the pills quickly, desperately trying not to lose one precious gram of DXM.

"Don't worry about it! You don't know what you're talking about," we insisted. "This is ours and you're our friend. You can stay or you can leave, it's your choice Kayla, but one thing is for sure the pills are staying."

Moments later, she left in disgust. We tried to convince her we were selling the pills, but in the days that followed we knew that she learned our secret and we couldn't fool her anymore. She cared for us and she didn't have many friends and neither did we. She could only see one possible outcome but knew us well enough to know that no matter what she attempted, we would do exactly what we wanted.

I didn't need to confess to her my reasons for wanting to die, but as each day grew closer to that outcome I confided in her. I had an endless stash of DXM and an endless stash of remorse and guilt. I knew that my brother was rotting away in prison and I was sure by now he had heard that I helped put him there. I was lost beyond belief and broken beyond repair. I wanted to erase the sins of my past so I could die in peace. I needed forgiveness but I found none.

By January, I was unrecognizable. For the past month, I had worn the same clothes that I had soiled with my bodily fluids. Day after day I consumed more pills, laying in my filth, waiting for my heart to stop beating and the pain of this life to slip away. With what started at 16 pills, then 32, now became 80 continually. I never expected it to take this long, most hours of the day I couldn't remember my name, how to smoke a cigarette or dial a number on the telephone. Sometimes my mind was clear, while other times my past crashed all around me as I screamed for mercy at the top of my lungs. I was a prisoner of my own personal hell, bound by my own destruction. I believed I was receiving exactly what I had deserved.

January 22, 2006

At my request, Kayla arranged for some friends to help carry me to an old Catholic Church late at night. It's the same Church I spent my youth in. I had so many vivid memories of that place. I was always taught that God was there and that He could easily be found. I was desperate enough to attempt anything to ease my conscience and erase my past. Like a crippled man they laid me on a Church pew and waited for me outside.

In that candle lit sanctuary, I turned my focus and all my attention to the numerous religious symbols and statues. I saw a statue of Mary, the mother of baby Jesus, pointing to the heavens as if telling me to pray. I saw gold and other statues of several canonized saints, marble floors, and could smell incense in the air.

"This is the perfect environment for God," I thought as I closed my eyes.

After several minutes of sitting there I felt nothing so I spoke: "God where are you? Are you here? Do you hear me?" As I spoke these words I felt a tear run down my cheeks. It was the first time I had cried in a long time. It was only one tear, but it was something. I spoke again, "God, I am lost and I blame you. I blame you for my past and I blame you for my situation. Why have you hidden yourself from me? Why don't you change me? I am lost and I am dying. I have hurt many people and now I am hurting myself..." I paused as if waiting for an answer that I knew wouldn't come. I then finished by saying, "it's all a big nothing and soon it will be finished."

Moments later my friends came to collect me jokingly asking how it went and if I found God. Looking into their eyes as they each helped stabilize me, I opened my mouth to speak.

"God is not here." I don't know why I said that, but I did. I wanted to say; "God is dead, or God is not real, or anything similar. Instead the phrase "God is not here" came from my lips and I didn't recant my statement.

I had searched and found nothing. I had questions, yet I received no answers. As they once again laid my destroyed body on the floor of the studio apartment I would never leave this floor again. I wasn't even 19 years old and I knew I was hours away from death. I had consumed more pills than I could count, committed more sins than I wanted to remember, and was weighed down by such enormous guilt. As I swallowed yet another dose of DXM, I was ready to die.

"...And the final condition of that man is worse than the first..."

- **Luke 11:24-28**

CHAPTER SIX:

God is real, God speaks, and God CAN hear me!

HROUGHOUT THE REST OF THE
NIGHT, after my failed attempt at
communicating with God, I swallowed pill
after pill. I wanted it to be over. I no longer
wanted to struggle. As the morning light broke
through the darkness of the curtains on the
windows, something birthed inside of me.

"I can't receive forgiveness from God, I can't
receive forgiveness from my incarcerated
brother, BUT maybe I can receive forgiveness
from my father."

On my hands and knees I crawled as if my
life depended on it. I had little time and only one
opportunity to receive some form of earthly
forgiveness. I didn't remember the last time I

had seen them or the last time we had spoken. I only remembered the shame I had caused them and how remorseful I was for my sins against them.

With each meter I passed, I felt my strength failing. I had nothing left, nothing left to offer my body except the thought of a possible forgiveness. Through forgiveness I might receive peace. Peace was the one thing I had searched for throughout my whole life. Peace was the one thing I desperately needed. In this moment, the need that gave my broken body strength was that hope for peace.

The closer I got to the store my father owned, the more strength I felt. Time was against me but I never lost hope. As soon as I saw the oversized glass windows of his store underneath the large painted sign, I had so much hope I could get off of my knees and stand up straight. Using the wall for support, I pressed on towards my goal.

Less than a meter from opening the front doors of the store, I wondered what words to use as I sought this possible forgiveness.

"What will I say to him? What can I say to him? Will he even recognize me? Will he even want me?"

All hope vanished when I saw my reflection through the window and remembered who I was. I was a monster, a drug addict, a criminal. I wasn't my father's son anymore. Knowing this hope didn't really exist, my body dropped to the floor. As my eyes closed, I allowed myself to finally surrender to the darkness.

Although the darkness was everywhere, my mind was clear. For the last several months, I couldn't think straight or have any real internal dialogue, but at this moment everything was different. I had a full understanding of the man I had become. I could reflect on every decision I had made since youth. As if watching my life from an outside perspective, I was desperately trying to get my other self to change the path leading me to this exact moment in time.

I could see how every decision led to this, my darkest moment. How every lie I told, every person I hurt, and everything I stole helped to shape me into the monster now lying out on the street. I felt like a garbage bag waiting to be picked up and tossed in a distant land fill out of sight and out of mind. How could I have gone this far? How could I have become so lost?

"I deserve this," I thought as I experienced a deep sinking feeling within me, "I know where I am going and I deserve this, I really do." At that moment I had accepted my fate. I accepted the reality I was now facing and knew I would be punished for my many sins.

In that moment, I accepted the total surrender of my life; the exact second I knew I was the only one responsible for the sins of my past, I felt a small yet real tugging on my heart. Only moments before this I felt a sinking sensation, but now something different was happening. I felt as if I was in the middle of two powerful forces, each force grabbing onto me like a gravitational pull absolutely beyond my control.

As the forces grew stronger and more intense, I felt as if I would shatter from the magnitude of it all. I quietly heard a whisper. It was a soft gentle voice that spoke. Even though it seemed distant something about the voice seemed familiar and commanded my full attention.

"Call on the name of Jesus," I heard. "Call on the name of Jesus."

I couldn't, even though I wanted to and knew I needed to. I pleaded with the voice - "I'm a monster, a drug addict, a criminal, I cannot. I am not able." I expected the soft voice to leave me in my distress but the voice did not.

The voice only continued and magnified. "Anyone who calls on the name of the Lord Jesus will be saved."

I saw another moment of hope, a moment of change, a moment of possibility. Reasoning with myself I pondered, "Could I really have hope? Could someone as lost as me be saved? Could I truly be forgiven?" As the two unseen forces continued their game of "tug of war" with me I made my decision. In desperation and with whatever strength and hope I had left I spoke three words: "Jesus save me!"

Instant transformation came upon me. I felt a presence of peace unlike I had never felt before. All pain, all worry and all regret left in the moment I spoke those three words. When the sinking feeling quickly stopped, a new feeling emerged. A feeling of rising came, rising towards a presence of radiant light. For the first time in my painful life, I felt love, peace, and mercy. I found everything I desperately sought after in the God I hated for so many years, the God Jesus the Christ!

I didn't see God, I didn't see angels and I didn't see family members who had died before me. I merely felt the conviction of sin, heard the words of truth and rested in the presence of the One who saved me. The peace I received seemed to last for hours. I didn't know if I was dead, alive, or dreaming, but I knew I didn't care. I was satisfied resting in the presence of great love.

As I opened my eyes the light changed, the presence changed and everything was different. I was now lying on a hospital bed attached to several machines with doctors surrounding me. Out of the corner of my eye I saw my mother crying but I could not hear her voice.

"Where am I? What are you doing to me? What happened?" I repeated hoping for answers.

As my eyes once again closed, I rested in the hospital bed. Several hours later I woke up in a calmer environment. I didn't understand where I was or what happened.

"Where I am? What happened to me?" I asked my mother.

"Chris you're very lucky, don't you remember anything?" said my mother through a facet of tears.

"I don't understand," I stated as the tears flowed from my eyes.

"We found you in the street. I bought you to the hospital. The doctors did as much as they could, but this is serious, I'm afraid there were some complications," She trembled. She asked, full of fear and desperation for answers, "What did you take? Why did you do this?"

I couldn't answer her; I couldn't even look at her. I knew how much I had hurt her.

"You were gone. I thought I had lost you," she said. "The doctors have begun some tests, and the results will come in the morning. Rest now, you need to rest," she continued.

"But mom I want to go home. I don't want to stay here," I pleaded. I felt afraid and out of control. In that moment I felt vulnerable.

"Chris you're sick, you need to stay here." And with that she left.

As I rested that night in my hospital bed, drifting in an out of sleep, I understood three things: God is real, God speaks, and God can hear me.

"It by grace you have been saved, through faith and this not from yourselves, it is the gift of God not by works, so that no one can boast."

- **Ephesians 2:8-9**

CHAPTER SEVEN:

Do You Want Coke or Sprite?

G OOD MORNING CHRIS. How are you feeling? My name is Doctor Snighter and I am the Hospital's Trauma Specialist."

Upon hearing these words, I attempted to sit upright giving the man my full attention and respect. I was eager to hear the results of the tests, but as I attempted the impossible, I quickly learned there was something wrong with my physical health.

I was still in constant pain from the weeks of self-inflected damage to my body. I knew something was different about my physical condition. For the past several weeks I could not properly urinate or have the full mobility of my limbs or speech. From the moment the doctor opened his mouth I saw the look on his face and feared for the worst.

"You wouldn't remember me but I was the initial doctor who treated you as your mother entered the hospital. There is no easy way to say this... You suffered major trauma to your brain and organs. Upon the results of the tests I'm afraid I must agree with the other doctors in charge of your long term health. From the MRI scans and blood results we have determined a very large percentage of your brain has suffered significant amounts of damage. We won't be certain as to the extent of the damage until after conducting more tests but we don't expect the results to be promising."

Hearing these words my heart stopped. "What have I done to myself?" I was hoping the fuzzy feeling in my brain was only temporary but now the doctors are taking away my hope, telling me I may never have the possibility of a normal life. If this wasn't bad enough, the doctors weren't even finished speaking. They let me have a moment to catch up before they continued.

"Your brain isn't our only concern. It's now been made evident that during your series of overdoses your kidneys have failed and there's a strong possibility they won't recover."

I wasn't even sure what a kidney was until the doctor continued with his diagnosis.

"We will schedule you to begin Dialysis treatment immediately to address any arising problems."

When he finally finished speaking, I was at a loss for words. I was more confused than when he first came in the room.

"I'm only a young man, this can't be possible. How could this happen to me?" In the mist of all my confusion I prayed, "Jesus, where are you?"

The doctors had given me devastating news and prepared me for a life of complete dependence on medical assistance. I didn't understand but I was preparing for dependence on something much greater than anything modern medicine. I was being molded to become dependent on Jesus.

Later that day as the doctors returned, I told them Jesus had saved me while in my coma. That He and He alone saved me from destruction and He had a special plan. Offended by my comment, Doctor Snighter replied: "I guess I did nothing to save you then? Maybe your Jesus doesn't need my help; maybe you don't need the medications that are keeping you from experiencing the full effects of your damage Chris."

Removing his elastic gloves, he left the room saying, "I have to attend to some other patients who need my help." And with that I was once again alone in my hospital room.

I wasn't given a Bible or a television. I was alone with my thoughts and isolated. The whole day I reflected more on the three things I knew for sure. God is real, God speaks and God can hear me. The more I devoured this simple truth the more I wondered: "If God is real, If God does speak and If God can hear me. THEN maybe God can speak to my body and heal me too." When I never thought that would be possible, but I believed God had a plan and He wasn't finished with His work.

All I ever wanted was to live a normal life. I wanted peace and the possibility to have a family. Right there in the simple hospital bed, facing challenges and physical impossibilities, I said three words: "Jesus Heal Me." I then rested hoping and praying tomorrow would be different.

Opening my eyes from the emptiness of the night, I could see the sun rising. It was beautiful and majestic. I've seen the sun rise many times but today it seemed different. Today it felt as though God had done it for me, if only to remind me that 'Even in our darkest hour, the light is still yet to come.'

As the nurse came in to deliver breakfast, I felt unusually hungry. I hadn't eaten real food in a long time. The food was your typical hospital food: cold, tasteless, and in small portions. However, I quickly thanked God for the ability to eat and then I attempted to sit-up for breakfast. From the moment my muscles contracted helping me to raise my upper body I felt it. I felt the life slowly returning. Raising the spoon of oatmeal to my lips I smiled at the nurse and she smiled back at me. Every bite of cold tasteless food that morning was a blessing.

Within the next several hours, all the doctors noticed my transformation. My body was showing signs of significant restoration. Later that night Doctor Snighter entered the room to have a conversation with me.

"Chris, I don't know what has happened in the last 24 hours but something has changed. Your body has completely restored itself on its own. The human body is a mysterious amazing evolution."

Smiling at Doctor Snighter I said, "The human body isn't as amazing as you say, but My

Jesus is more amazing than my words can possibly describe."

He didn't argue with me. We both had our separate beliefs but we agreed on one thing - I was ready to be released from the Trauma unit and be discharged from Intensive Care.

After all the paperwork was finalized, the nurses handed me the clothes and belongings I entered the hospital with. Thankfully they had washed the dirty rags I was wearing so the smell of urine and vomit had washed away. While gazing into the mirror, I wasn't exactly pleased with my reflection. I had spent the last several years as a hopeless dope addict and the scars had not been magically removed. However, I smiled and said "Chris, you are not the man who came into this hospital on a stretcher. You are different, you are known by God."

My mother was there waiting for me. She wanted to help support me embrace this new chapter in my life. Looking over my left shoulder, I saw a vending machine selling Coca-Cola. I thought it would be nice to enjoy a cold soft drink before entering the car and I asked my mother if she had any extra coins. As she searched in her purse for a dollar to purchase the drink I placed my hands in my pockets. In my left pocket, next to a couple random coins and pieces of paper, was something I didn't recognize.

Pulling the object out to examine it, I noticed right away what it was. It was the cross broken off from my mother's favorite rosary. Without giving it any thought I reached out my hand. "Here mom, I think this is yours," I said while placing the miniature cross in her loving hand.

"Where did you get this?" she asked as I pointed to my pocket. "I was praying with this the day we found you in the street, I don't understand how you got this."

After a brief pause I replied "I don't know mom, it was just there". As I reached the vending machine, I turned slightly and asked, "Do you want Coke or Sprite?"

"He was pierced for our transgressions, He was crushed for our iniquities; the punishment that brought us peace was upon Him, and by His wounds we are healed."
-                    **Isaiah 53:5**

CHAPTER EIGHT:

Time to Make a Choice

O KAY CHRIS, YOUR MOTHER AND I have made all the arrangements we just need your signature here." My father encouraged me while he placed the tip of his black ink pen on the desired line.

It's called the Ben Franklin close. According to physiologic studies, by placing your pen on the exact place in the contract you want someone to sign, they're more likely to not back out of the sale. Whoever proctored that study didn't use test subjects like me.

Today was the day I was scheduled to go to a Christian Discipleship School called Teen Challenge. I have heard many things about this school, but what scared me the most was the required commitment. The school was a minimum of 18 months of intense Physical,

Mental, and Spiritual training. If asked to sum up everything I had heard about this program in one word I would have chosen the word, Sacrifice.

"Chris this is the logical next step for you. Last week you were in the hospital, now you desperately need a good foundation," my mother said.

She was right. I had only been a 'Christian' less than a full week and did not understand what I would do with my new freedom. Everything inside of me screamed "Go to Teen Challenge" and for several nights, my dreams continuously pointed me there. However, at this moment my only thoughts were "18 months? No freedom, No contact with women, no right to make my own decisions, for 18 months? Why would I possibly consider this as an option?"

As I reached for the pen my father had placed on the application, I froze. I quickly retracted my hand, raised my head towards my father, and said, "I can't do it, I'm sorry I wasted your time." I then walked out of my family's home. Once again I had made a bad decision out of fear and uncertainty and the unwillingness to fully surrender myself.

Instead of choosing an 18-month Christian Discipleship program I chose instead another easy 30-Day Rehab center. I convinced myself that I just needed a safe place to get my life together, to develop the proper life skills needed to stay clean and sober. I convinced myself to believe a lie, but deep down I knew the truth. I knew I needed help beyond drug addiction. Only a fool would believe my root issues were the drug abuse. I had a spiritual disease, one that required treatment, yet I refused to take the medicine I needed and address my real issues.

Upon arrival at yet another inpatient Rehab facility, I desperately tried to learn. I wanted a better life. A life without slavery to the addictions I faced within me. I worked harder and invested myself in the program more than any other. When the required Alcoholics Anonymous meeting was three times a week, I attended 3 per day. Constantly I volunteered and did everything within my ability to fully commit to this 30-day program.

The program was just like the others I had been to group therapy, individual therapy, group meetings, and plenty of smoke breaks. We were a bunch of sick individuals, living in a community, trying to achieve the impossible. Every day we would confess. We confessed to being hopeless drug addicts and alcoholics. Our only goal was to survive 24 hours at a time and for a while this helped to quench the thirst of our addictions. But like that beach ball held under water, I knew a time would soon come when everything would violently emerge.

"We are so proud of you Chris." My parents said as we celebrated my sixth month anniversary of being clean and sober together.

"I knew you could do it. You have a wonderful job, you're making honest money, and you have a whole future ahead of you," my grandmother said as she held me and gently kissed my cheek. Everyone was so happy. Everyone was so proud. Everyone except me. Inside I was ashamed and living a lie.

Two days before this celebration, I had consumed alcohol with some old friends from the neighborhood. Because I was living in a sober community, I forced myself to keep this secret in fear I would be sent back to Rehab. Not being able to live with the guilt, I wrote a suicide note and secretly left in the middle of the night. I felt I let everyone down and believed their lives would be better without me.

Within the hour I had consumed enough alcohol and narcotics to ease my fears and do what I thought was necessary. The police, my family, and my friends were all searching for me. They knew what I was capable of and they understood my time was limited before I would accept a permanent solution to a temporary problem.

Driving around in the truck my boss had graciously allowed me to use, I went out to an old abandoned road. I could see no one for miles. After putting the vehicle in park, I calmly reached for a bottle of pills a doctor had given me. Demerol, a strong pain medication, was my vehicle of choice; one that would take me out of this world and away from this pain. In-between each prayer and each sob I swallowed another pill.

"Why God? Why? Why save me and then leave me?" I asked as I swallowed another pill. "You revealed yourself in power and then left me in my mess! What type of savior would do that?" Another pill down. "I'll be coming to you soon. Take care of my family, take care of me." The combination of prayers and narcotics continued throughout the whole night until collapsing on the dirt road and passing out to the sound of my own weeping.

The next morning I opened my eyes only to discover I was covered in mud, with bugs crawling all over my body.

"Where did these scars come from?" I thought as I stumbled my way back to the Truck. "I need your help, I need you." I continued to pray out loud. Suddenly I felt as if someone was speaking behind me.

"Tell them the truth," I heard as I turned around to see who was speaking. To my surprise no one was there. I was all alone on this dirt road, alone and confused.

Calling a friend from the sober community, I confessed everything and accepted the offer to be brought to a hospital to help regain stabilization. Throughout the week of detox I had many visitors coming to help make sure they knew I still had their support. Family, friends, but also someone I didn't expect to see, my boss.

The moment that large burley man saw me, he calmly walked over and embraced me.

"You had us all worried young man. You had me worried," Al said and he was checking to make sure everything was all right with me. "My Church and I were praying for you. Don't worry about anything. You didn't lose your job; I am just so happy you're still with us," he said moments before he left. He was late on a delivery, a delivery I should have made but couldn't because I was in the hospital.

While I didn't know he was a Christian, I always thought something was different about him because he was good and genuinely cared about my life. He showed an interest and took me under his wing. My only regret now is how I took advantage of his good nature for so many months while dealing with my own personal struggles.

Throughout that whole year, my life was an absolute disaster. I had no foundation and couldn't keep my life from falling apart. Every time I would stay sober for 30 days, I would instantly fall apart again and need someone to help put me back together. Overdose after overdose, failure after failure, lie after lie. Nothing was working and my situation was only growing worse.

"Do you know why you are here Mr. Buscher?" Judge Laddusaw asked while sitting in his black robes about to pronounce his judgment on my life.

They walked me before his pulpit in chains. In the last year I had overdosed several times, been arrested for petty crimes, and hospitalized for self-inflected suicide attempts. Now I was on trial for my mental stability, to see if I was a threat to society.

"Over the last several years I have watched you. I have watched you from the newspapers and from the eyes of your family. I have heard more stories about you than I care to remember. It will sadden my wife when I inform her you were before me today in my court once again. My wife cared for you as you were her child and she always saw great potential in you."

His words quickly gained my attention. I'd been here before but never was I spoken to in this way. I was used to being treated as an animal they didn't know what to do with, but here, in front of this Judge, I was human.

"Your brother Joey was before me only months ago. When he was sentenced, I knew you would be affected as well. No one in this room doubts the pain and suffering you have had in your life, nor can we ignore the pain and suffering you have inflected on others."

After saying these words, he bowed his head as if he listening for what to say next. It seemed as if he was praying for wisdom. Everyone, including the officers who held my chains, waited with anticipation for his judgment.

After moments of awkward silence passed through the heavy air that filled the court room, we all heard these words: "Mr. Buscher, stand before me."

As I rose to my feet, the sound of the chains on my wrists and ankles echoed throughout the court room.

"If I thought even for a moment that a Rehab facility would somehow fix you, I would send you there. If I thought another prison wouldn't completely destroy you, I would send you there. You have been presented with a wonderful opportunity to voluntarily enter a Christian Discipleship program called Teen Challenge. I am very familiar with this program and their tremendous success with graduating students. This school would completely change your life."

Clearing his throat he continued, "I know the reason you won't go is because you're afraid. You are full of fear and you have been full of fear your whole life. If I sent you there on a court order you would only escape as soon as your first opportunity. So I will give you a choice. As of today you must decide your future. Either you will choose to voluntarily graduate the Teen Challenge program or I will sentence you to the next six months in a mental health facility for evaluation and assessment of your chronic situation." With that, he cleared the room and gave me time to make my choice.

Something was different about today. On this day I felt my eyes open. The words the judge had spoken where not his own and we all knew it. These were the words I had been waiting for and exactly the words I needed to hear. I looked at my father as I was escorted out of the room. With a single tear in my eye I said: "I am ready, call Teen Challenge."

"For though a righteous man falls seven times, he rises again, but the wicked are brought down by calamity."

-           **Proverbs 24:16**

CHAPTER NINE:

Sweet Surrender

January 23, 2007
5:00 A.M.

W AKE UP CHRIS, WAKE UP!" My father said as he shook me out of my slumber.

Quickly glancing at the nearby window, I could see the sun hadn't even risen. Still halfway intoxicated from the night before, I reached for my cigarettes to have my morning smoke. "You won't need any of those today." He said as he smashed my last package of Marlboros.

Having spent the whole night gorging myself with narcotics and alcohol trying to forget what the morning would bring - I did almost forget – I begrudgingly got out of bed. Unbeknownst to me, this was exactly one year from the day of my salvation. Exactly one year since Jesus had shown me mercy during a near fatal drug overdose. It was the day I was scheduled to enter Teen Challenge of the Midlands in Colfax, Iowa.

From the moment I got there, change took place. It wasn't an instant miracle, but it was little things happening all around and within me. I saw that everything that had happened throughout my existence had a purpose, and that God in His infinite wisdom, had brought me to this place.

Stepping out of my father's minivan, I remember vividly seeing the entry door of the four story compound. It was as if I had seen it before, not in any photos or stories I had heard. No, this was very different. I had seen this many times in my dreams. Normally the first several hours of withdrawal would be unbearable. I expected to be sick; I expected my disease to begin to violently drag me back to the streets. But the painful withdraws never came and through this it was made abundantly clear - I was standing on Holy ground.

While everyone came for a variety of personal reasons, the people here were very different. There was joy in their eyes and they had a sense of clarity about them. Having completed over eight Rehab facilities prior to entering Teen Challenge, something about this place struck me as odd. No one asked me what type of drugs I had been addicted to or what variety of medications I needed. They only were concerned with two questions: 'Do you know Jesus, and does Jesus know you?'

That first night as I laid my head on my pillow, I pulled the blanket over my face and quietly thanked God for bringing me here.

"Jesus, I want what they have, I want to know you. Please Lord, I want to experience you." And with those simple words I finished my prayer, laid down, and slept in peace. It was the first night in years that I could sleep without the help of medicine.

"Towel time!" A man yelled as the lights suddenly came on. Fast. Everyone sprang from there bed and rushed towards the showers. It was exactly 6:00 a.m. and we had only 15 minutes to shower, shave, dress, and organize our bed before marching down the stairs to begin our daily agenda of what many called: "Bible Boot Camp".

Every second of every day was completely and thoroughly organized. We had corporate prayers and Bible study before breakfast, then immediately following was a scheduled Church service that all the staff and students attended daily. The church service comprised some songs of worship and messages delivered by a Pastor, a staff member, and sometimes even a student. Everyone seemed to intimately know Jesus and devoured every page of the Bible.

There was no band, no choir and no famous musician playing his guitar. They played a CD as people either raised their hands to sing or fell on their knees at the altars. Students would each pray for each other. They knew each other's needs and held hands thanking Jesus for everything good and bad in their lives. The situation I found myself in was unlike anything in other churches; this was undefiled religion in its purest form.

After Chapel, our day was equally divided between physical labor and Biblical studies. The school resided on over 90 acres of land and the building itself was rather large. Each of us had a responsibility to maintain the property and learned valuable skills while doing so. We poured our sweat and blood into that place; every moment we increasingly learned more about ourselves and our potential.

Biblical studies involved corporate lectures and personal devotions. Within the first six months I was given a better quality Biblical education than many pastors and ministers serving throughout the Kingdom. But knowledge and information wasn't the secret to the success of the Teen Challenge School. Establishing personal relationships with Jesus and learning how to hear the voice of the Holy Spirit was what really changed the lives of these desperate men. Many would come here as homeless junkies like me but would later graduate as strong men of God, destined to turn the world upside-down.

"Chris, it's time to meet the reverend." I heard as I was splitting wood behind the barn. I had spent the last three hours lifting the heavy logs onto the splitter and my muscles were screaming for a break.

"Okay, I'm coming brother," I said as I finished my last log and walked towards the main building. I had never met the Reverend Larry Low before, but the other students spoke about him with great respect.

Walking up the hill towards the front door, I brushed as much as the dirt off my body as possible. During the last few hours of lifting broken tree limbs and splitting the wood into smaller pieces, I had got very dirty.

"I wonder what my first meeting will be like." I thought as I climbed the stairs to his office.

"Come in, come in," I heard a calm voice say from behind a wooden door.

The old bearded man had a smile on his face that could brighten even the darkest of situations. There was something peaceful about him and something intriguing about the presence in that simple room.

"I was just praying for you Chris." He said as he directed me to sit in a chair that was adjacent to his. "Are you ready to begin to learn how to hear from the Holy Spirit?" he asked as he started deep into my eyes.

"I don't know Reverend," I said with doubt and disbelief. "To be honest Reverend, I'm not much of a charismatic person. Don't be offended, but I'm not as crazy as some of these people." After saying these words, I halfway expected a lecture or at least a negative remark from him.

Instead he laughed, "Don't worry, I'm not crazy either. Shall we begin?"

Nodding in response, I focused on the Reverend.

"I want you to close your eyes, rest for a moment, and clear your mind of all thoughts. Don't attempt to bring any memory or thought into your conscience, just rest," he said in a peaceful voice.

I found this was difficult. I was nervous and could never rest my weary mind. However, after several minutes of silence it began. He must have known I was calm and relaxed because he then continued by praying: "Lord Jesus, show Chris what you want him to see."

I didn't see angels or receive a prophetic message wrote in a distant sky. I saw a memory, a strange memory I couldn't understand and never thought about prior to this.

"I don't think this is working Reverend," I said with even more doubt than before. "I see..." as I attempted to tell him what I was seeing, he quickly stopped me and said.

"Don't tell me what you see. I don't need to know. Simply tell Jesus how you feel when you see this memory."

"How did he know I was seeing a memory? Why didn't he want to hear it? What type of therapy is this?" I thought after hearing his lack of interest in my memory.

After a moment I uttered "Lord Jesus, I feel confused. I don't understand why I am seeing this memory. It honestly doesn't mean anything to me."

The memory I saw was from the day I was discharged from the Hospital and found my mother's cross in my pocket; a simple cross broken off of her rosary. "Why this memory? Why not deal with a truly damaging memory - like the trauma of my past?" I thought after I prayed.

"Calm yourself brother and just listen. Listen to His voice. He will speak if you listen," Reverend Larry said. He must have seen my discomfort as I wrestled with my thoughts.

Once again, I tried to calm myself and prayed, "Lord Jesus, I am confused I want to hear your truth." Instantly within myself I could feel the answers. I heard no mysterious voice but I felt the answers and I knew it was Jesus speaking.

"I brought you to me and I have been with you always. There was never a moment that I had left you alone. The day I made myself known to you was the day you started to listen. You have heard many things about me from many people who don't know me. They have taught you religion and shown you symbols in an attempt to find me. I broke my cross off your mother's religious rosary and gently placed it in your pocket. I did this."

As soon as the voice spoke within my heart, tears streamed down my face. I was being washed with the word of God and being cleansed of all of the lies.

"But why God, why did you bring me here?" I continued to pray through the tears.

"You are mine and I want you to know me. Just as I broke the cross away from the religious symbol, I brought you here to remove you from the religious ideas of others. Focus on me, focus on my cross, and focus on my words. Lose all religion to find me"

I can't imagine what the Reverend must have been thinking seeing me weep before the Lord's presence. I could hear him quietly in the background praising the Lord for piercing my heart with this truth. The Reverend never knew what the Lord and I discussed, he only knew the Lord was speaking.

Before leaving the Reverend's office, I finally understood what his job at Teen Challenge was. His job wasn't to console or help solve the problems of my past. His job was something simpler yet more profound. His job was only to arrange the meeting with the healer and to teach me to listen to His voice.

Upon hearing the Lord speak, I became addicted to his presence. All day and all night I engaged with Him. Jesus became the reason I woke up every morning and the reason behind my every decision. I wanted so much to give Him glory and truly serve Him. I found my heart breaking for the lost souls and even the people inside the churches who didn't have what I had. I wanted to spread the word Jesus. I wanted to make a difference. "But who am I?" I thought. "I'm nobody. I'm 20-years-old. Who would listen to me?"

Within the following months, I refused to wait for things to happen. Many people were telling me, "Just wait on the Lord. Simply wait Chris. Things will happen in its time." Somehow, even with my lack of experience I knew they were wrong. Good things happen to those who wait, but the problem with most people waiting is that they become inactive while waiting for their opportunity. They never truly understand until after all the opportunities passed by them. I saw it in too many people and the more I studied the Bible and Church history, the more I was convinced and compelled to not allow this to happen.

I took an honest look at the situation I found myself in. I was still only a student of a Christian Discipleship school, yet I was surrounded by people who needed me as much as I needed them. I fully invested myself into them, praying with them, encouraging them, and daily ministering to them as they did the same for me. We became a band of brothers preparing for our moment to turn the world upside-down. We fully understood this season of our lives was only the beginning; it was only training, only preparation.

The night before my graduation from Teen Challenge, I was nervous. I had spent the last 18-months devoted to serving and laboring with Jesus. I knew God was calling me to ministry and I fully knew that many difficult times would come before me. Praying how Reverend Larry Low had taught me I said: "Jesus, thank you, thank you for everything. You have healed me, you have cleaned me, you have separated me from this world to sit at your feet and learn from you. Tomorrow I will once again venture out into this world. Hold on to me, hold on to me. No matter what comes my way, stay with me and never let me run too far away that you can't bring me home. Here I am, God; your faithful, humble servant. Use me."

After speaking that prayer with my whole heart, I once again laid my head on my pillow and drifted away into a peaceful sleep. The Lord has always spoken through His Holy Bible and sometimes in my past, when I desperately needed Him, He would speak through my dreams. This was one of those nights where I was about to make another life decision- stepping out into the world of the unknown where I desperately needed his presence.

A reoccurring dream that started as a young child and lasted throughout my entire life came again that night. The dream has always been the same and always as vivid as the first occurrence. This dream gave me the needed strength to carry on, to continue believing, and to keep fighting the good fight of faith.

Trapped in absolutely darkness, I have a state of consciousness but no form. I have no physical body; only an existent spirit and I'm surrounded by a deep understanding that I'm not alone here. There is a multitude of others facing the same exact situation; we are all waiting to be selected and to be chosen.

At the perfect time, I am carried towards the light and seated in a presence that overwhelms me. The presence is Majestic and holy; yet it's loving and patient. I'm being shown several options and am given many lives to choose from. The details of each life are never clear; the only thing I understand is that I must make my final decision. With complete certainty, I make my decision and declared, "This one, I choose this one"

"Are you sure," the Spirit asked. "This life will bring me great glory, yet your life will be filled with pain and suffering," the Spirit continued. "Are you sure," the Spirit inquired for the final time.

"Yes," I replied and instantly I am born.

"Your young men will see visions... I will pour out my Spirit in those days."
-                                **Joel 2:27-29**

ABOUT THE AUTHOR

Chris Buscher is the inspirational co-founder and CEO of Lay me Down Ministry who after a tumultuous childhood and years of looking for peace, found it in the words of Jesus Christ. Christ became more than just words for Chris, he was love, mercy, and compassion through the power of his gospel. A gospel that after Chris experiences a prophetic dream in college, felt the needed to share with the world!

Since then, Chris has traveled the world sharing his story about how he was healed and given a new life by the ways of Jesus Christ. Chris is no fly-by-night preacher. He's given up everything he owned and left his family to tell others what faith and Jesus can do in their lives. Chris has ministered in numerous nations and today his company Lay Me Down Ministry is operating in a total of three different continents and consists of over 120 pastors and 65 churches. Lay Me Down Ministry is completely united with one powerful goal in mind: raising the next generation of world changing Christians!

Chris Buscher is also the writer of numerous inspirational books such as *My Confession*, *Hashtag Faith*, *Take Up Your Cross*, and MANY more. You can find his publications on Amazon or directly through his different publishers at UP Books, LMDM Publishing House, and Generational Publishing.

Made in the USA
Middletown, DE
14 December 2015